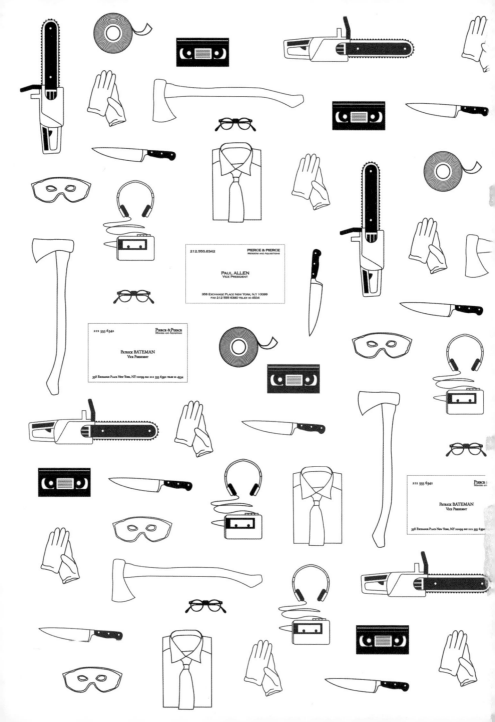

AMERICAN
PSYCHO

How to Make a Killing
in Business...and Life

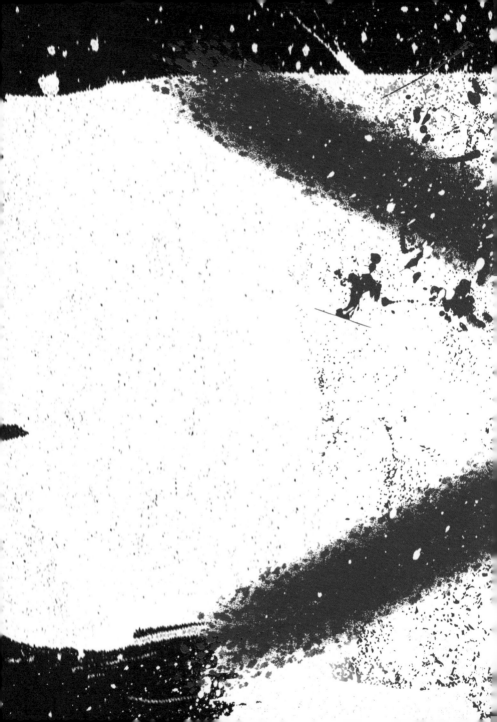

AMERICAN PSYCHO

How to Make a Killing in Business ... and Life

Patrick Bateman,
as told to Robb Pearlman

RIZZOLI UNIVERSE

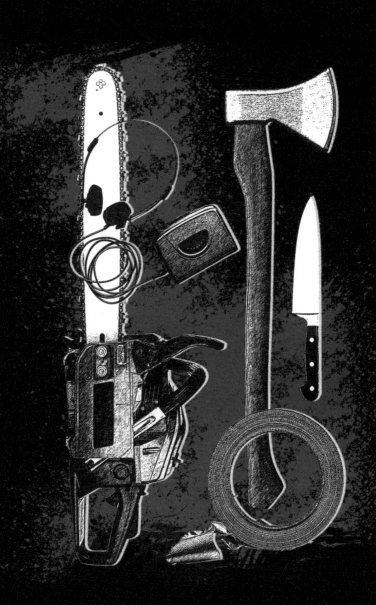

CONTENTS

FOREWORD

I LIVE IN THE AMERICAN GARDENS BUILDING ON West 81st Street on the 11th floor. My name is Patrick Bateman. You may have heard of me. But did you hear that I'm utterly insane? Here's the thing: you're not terribly important to me, but I know that I'm important to you. Important enough for you to buy this book. I guess I should thank you for that. So, because I understand why you'd want to be me, here's what I'm going to do: I'm going to tell you how to be just like me. But before we get started, you should know that there is an idea of a Patrick Bateman. Some kind of abstraction. But there is no real me.

"I have all the characteristics of a human being: flesh, blood, skin, hair. And I take care of it."

SKIN DEEP

1

PUTTING YOUR BEST (HUMAN) FACE FORWARD

- Start by eating a balanced diet and following my routine: In the morning, if my face is a little puffy, I'll put on an ice pack while doing my stomach crunches. I can do 1000 now. After I remove the ice pack, I use a deep pore cleanser lotion. In the shower, I use a water-activated gel cleanser, then a honey almond body scrub, and on the face an exfoliating gel scrub. Then I apply an herb-mint facial mask, which I leave on for ten minutes while I prepare the rest of my routine. I always use an aftershave lotion with little or no alcohol because alcohol dries your face out and makes you look older. Then moisturizer, then an anti-aging eye balm followed by a final moisturizing protective lotion.

♣ Maintaining a killer body will give you stamina for long days in the office, and enough energy for a variety of physically demanding after-work and extracurricular activities. A rigorous physical wellness regimen—including but not limited to activities like exercising at home in your underwear, boxing at The Harvard Club, or running to your office—will release tension, help you look better in a suit, and keep your blood flowing.

You can always be thinner, better.

"I am only
an entity.
Something
illusory."

2

DRESS TO KILL

Keep up to date on the latest trends, but don't lose your head over fashion. There are definite dos and don'ts to wearing a bold-striped shirt—anyone knows a bold-striped shirt calls for solid colored or discreetly pattered suits and ties.

- When going for a haircut or shave, always tip the stylist 15%, unless your stylist is the owner of the salon, in which case you shouldn't tip anything at all. And tell them Patrick sent you.

- When paired with a killer smile, sunglasses, especially indoors, and particularly at work, are always a good idea.

While menswear and grooming have been elevated and embraced by society in recent years, your single straight male colleagues will always look to someone who cuts a swath through the office as well as you for good fashion advice. But you can't spend all day on the phone making their decisions for them without severely impeding your own productivity or suffocating their individual sense of style. Cut to the heart of the matter and give them some basic bullet points, like suggesting Oliver Peoples glasses and Valentino Couture that is cut proportionately and according to their physique. Don't let them touch the watch.

"I do not have
a single, clear,
identifiable
emotion, except
for greed
and disgust.
Something
horrible is
happening inside
of me and I don't
know why."

3
MIND GAMES

Problems always seem worse than they are at night, so don't shoot your mouth off or do anything that will push you or your career over the edge. Wait until the morning, take a shower, and then reflect on the problem. It'll probably go away on its own.

- Old habits die hard, so acknowledge that your behavior can be erratic sometimes.

- It's not the '80s anymore, so you can totally lean into the whole Yale thing.

Being a child of divorce doesn't excuse everything, but you can use it as an excuse for some things.

Be a happy camper! When you feel like you're at the end of your rope, relax by doing the crossword.

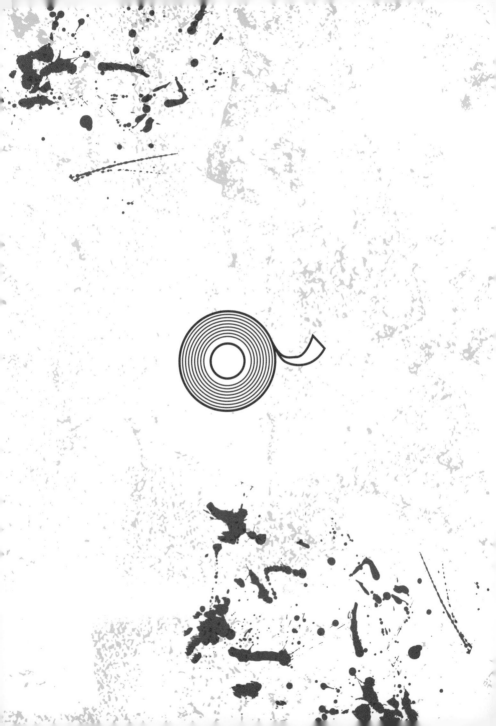

"I'm just
a happy
camper!
Rockin' and
a-rollin'!"

● Wearing headphones can provide a soundtrack to your day, while also blocking out unwanted conversations or homicidal thoughts.

● Some people bind and gag their inner turmoil by practicing meditation. Sit with your eyes closed and concentrate on your breathing or repeat two of my favorite mantras:
  • I simply am not there.
  • There are no more barriers to cross. All I have in common with the uncontrollable and the insane, the vicious and the evil, all the mayhem I have caused and my utter indifference toward it, I have now surpassed.

PIERCE & PIERCE
MERGERS AND AQUISITIONS

212.555.6342

PAUL ALLEN
VICE PRESIDENT

ACE NEW YORK, N.Y 10099
90 TELEX IO 4534

35

212 555 6342

PIERCE & PIERCE
MERGERS AND AQUISITIONS

PATRICK BATEMAN
VICE PRESIDENT

358 EXCHANGE PLACE NEW YORK, NY 10099 FAX 212 555 6390 TELEX IO 4534

"My nightly
bloodlust has
overflown
into my days.
I feel lethal,
on the verge
of frenzy."

IT'S A CUTTHROAT BUSINESS

THE FIRST PAPER CUT IS THE DEEPEST

You only get one chance to make a first impression. There's no better way to come out guns blazing than with a finely crafted business card. Bone with Silian Rail is nice. Eggshell with Romalian type? Better. Raised lettering, pale nimbus, white. Think of the hand feel. The tasteful thickness of it. And if, oh my god, it even has a *watermark . . . ?*

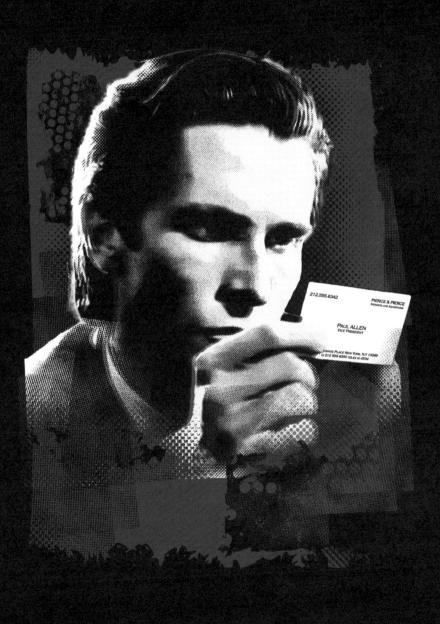

PIERCE & PIERCE
Mergers and Acquisitions

212.555.6342

PAUL ALLEN
VICE PRESIDENT

␣␣ANGE PLACE NEW YORK, N.Y 10089
␣L 212 555 6280 TELEX 10 4534

Take a stab at building a good relationship with your assistant. Because you're going to have to see them every workday, sometimes more, the relationship will work best if you're able to assert a sense of dominance early on, so they know their place. It helps if you can find someone young, moldable, and easy on the eyes, too. Unfortunately, none of those attributes are listed on a resume, so you'll really only get a sense of how you'll get along, and how much you may be able to get away with before HR is involved, during the interview process.

Tastes may vary, but I bet a young woman like my assistant, Jean, may check all of those boxes for you. She must dress, if she's pretty, in a dress or skirt and not some boxy business suit. This will also make it easier to take her out to dinner as a reward for hard work. As a boss and a mentor, it's your responsibility to inspire her to be the best she can be for you.

"I'm into Murders and Executions mostly."

- Your assistant should always know your schedule, how to respond meeting or social invitations, and how to handle unexpected visitors. Ask them to make your dining reservations and appointments so they know all about the trendy locations you frequent, and just enough about your time out of the office to make them as envious as they are curious about your personal life. This will simultaneously dissuade them from stabbing you in the back (at least until you stab them first!), while showing her that you are every bit as big a deal as they think you are.

- Don't forget, you have a lunch meeting with Cliff Huxtable at the Four Seasons in 20 minutes.

When having a business lunch, mirror the physical movements of the person you're meeting with. They'll see you as being on their side when you're really killing them with kindness just long enough to get what you want.

I SIMPLY AM NOT THERE

Like a slaughterhouse processing tons of meat annually, corporations can churn through dozens of employees every fiscal year. It can be practically impossible to remember everyone, let alone care enough about them to notice when they're gone. Your colleagues, however, should all know who you are. But if a colleague mistakes you for someone else—even if that someone is an idiot—don't take immediate action. Rather than biting their head off, gather enough embarrassing personal and professional ammunition to humiliate them at a later date. This means disarm them with charm until you're ready to stick the knife in.

CONFLICT REVOLUTION

● Office politics and situations aren't always as black and white (or black and blue, depending on how rough you get) as they seem. Having a frank and honest discussion with your coworker, in a neutral setting such as a restroom, might bring peace and help put things to permanent rest.

- If a colleague has wronged you, shoot them! An *email*, ha ha. If that doesn't work, report them to HR.

- Whether dealing with business associates or your attorney, remember that communications about especially serious matters can have especially serious consequences. Because tone, context, and an appropriate sense of urgency may be lost in a text or email, it's sometimes better to leave a detailed voicemail.

● Money talks and everyone has their price. So, before you pull the trigger on any deal, always negotiate for the best terms.

● Sometimes, it becomes clear that an argument is going nowhere. Never beat a dead horse. Leave. I assess the situation and go.

"I think
my mask
of sanity
is about
to slip."

WHEN WORK BLEEDS INTO PERSONAL LIFE

- Though I can hide my cold gaze, and you can shake my hand and feel flesh gripping yours, and maybe you can even sense our lifestyles are probably comparable.

- While your office may primarily be a place of business, it can also be a safe space for you to celebrate after setting the world on fire—or to take cover after things crash down on your head.

- It's always better to kill two birds with one stone: Social events should be more than opportunities to just shoot the breeze. They're good for mulling over business problems, examining opportunities, exchanging rumors, and spreading gossip.

- Work friends may not always be the same as real friends (whatever those are), but they can be a means to an end. Find out as much as possible about the people you work with: where they went to school, their favorite spots, who they're dating, etc. Bank all of these details about the lives of your coworkers for when you can use them to your advantage, or are questioned about their whereabouts.

● Don't let anyone twist your arm to get you to drive them to the airport. But if you want to lay the groundwork for some future arm twisting of your own, bite the bullet and offer to help them pack for their trip. Do note that Jean Paul Gaultier makes the best overnight bags.

● Know where the bodies are buried. There's no better leverage than knowledge—especially knowledge you aren't supposed to have.

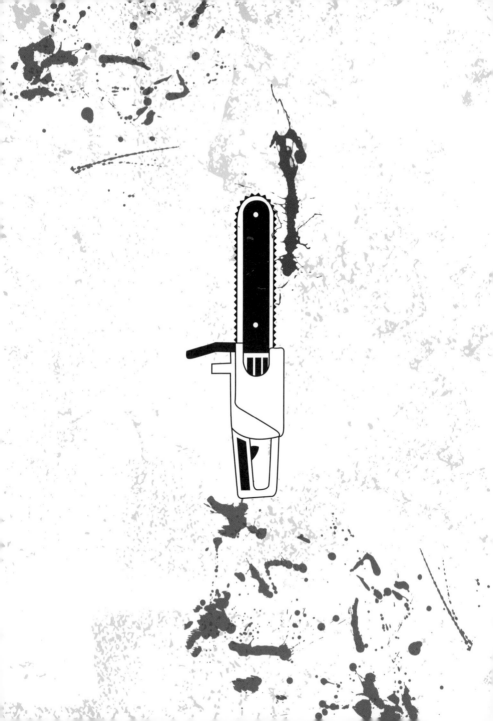

"I need to engage in engage in homicidal behavior on a massive scale."

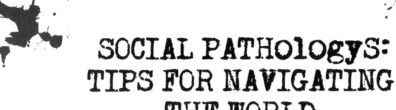

SOCIAL PATHOLOGYS: TIPS FOR NAVIGATING THE WORLD OF OTHER PEOPLE

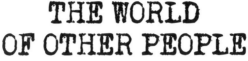

HOME-ICIDAL TENDENCIES

- Cover your tracks! Being disrespectful of someone's home is an assault on their, and your, personal integrity. Always use a coaster when setting a beverage or sorbet carton down on a coffee table in a friend or coworker's apartment. Wear a mask (even if you're not sick) or other protective clothing such as a poncho or raincoat, take off your shoes, and do whatever you can not to make a mess. In fact, the best way to be a good guest, especially if the host isn't there at the time, is to make it seem as if you never were either.

Know when it's time to leave. And when it's time for others to leave. Especially if they don't want to get hurt.

2

DON'T BE A CONVERSATION KILLER

● Small talk can be murder, especially if you're out with people you just spent eight hours with at the office. Keep things moving and pepper the conversation with little known facts or trivia about the things you care about, like current events, song lyrics, or quotes from serial killers.

◆ Here are some potential talking points:

WAR AND PIECE

"Now that apartheid is over, or at least out of fashion, we must focus our political attentions toward efforts concerning slowing down the nuclear arms race, stopping terrorism, and world hunger. We have to provide food and shelter for the homeless, and oppose racial discrimination and promote civil rights, while also promoting equal rights for women. We have to encourage a return to traditional moral values. Most importantly, we have to promote general social concern and less materialism in young people."

KILLER TUNES

"I've been a big Genesis fan ever since the release of their 1980 album, *Duke*. Before that, I really didn't understand any of their work. Too artsy, too intellectual. It was on *Duke* where Phil Collins's presence became more apparent. I think *Invisible Touch* was the group's undisputed masterpiece. It's an epic meditation on intangibility. At the same time, it deepens and enriches the meaning of the preceding three albums. Listen to the brilliant ensemble playing of Banks, Collins, and Rutherford. You can practically hear every nuance of every instrument. In terms of lyrical craftsmanship, the sheer songwriting, this album hits a new peak of professionalism. Take the lyrics to 'Land of Confusion.' In this song, Phil Collins addresses the problems of abusive political authority. 'In Too Deep' is the most moving pop song of the 1980s, about monogamy and commitment. The song is extremely uplifting. Their lyrics are as positive and affirmative as anything I've heard in rock. Phil Collins's solo career seems to be more commercial and therefore more satisfying, in a narrower way. Especially songs like 'In the Air Tonight' and 'Against All Odds.' But I also think Phil Collins works best within the confines of the group, than as a solo artist, and I stress the word artist. 'Sussudio' is a great, great song, a personal favorite."

"You like Huey Lewis and The News?"

"I love Huey Lewis and The News. Their early work was a little too new wave for my tastes, but when *Sports* came out in '83, I think they really came into their own, commercially and artistically. The whole album has a clear, crisp sound, and a new sheen of consummate professionalism that really gives the songs a big boost. He's been compared to Elvis Costello, but I think Huey has a far more bitter, cynical sense of humor. . . . In '87, Huey released this, *Fore*, their most accomplished album. I think their undisputed masterpiece is 'Hip to be Square,' a song so catchy, most people probably don't listen to the lyrics. But they should, because it's not just about the pleasures of conformity, and the importance of trends, it's also a personal statement about the band itself."

"Though it may be hard to choose a favorite among so many great tracks on Whitney Houston's debut album, it's clear that 'The Greatest Love of All' is one of the best, most powerful songs ever written about self-preservation and dignity. Its universal message crosses all boundaries and instills one with the hope that it's not too late to better ourselves. Since it's impossible in this world we live in to empathize with others, we can always empathize with ourselves. It's an important message, crucial really. And it's beautifully stated on the album."

DORSIA

"Try
getting a
reservation
at Dorsia
now!"

PAINT THE TOWN BLOOD RED

● Assess the situation and go.

● Traffic can be killer during rush hour, so give yourself plenty of time to make your reservation at Espace. But if you still find yourself stuck in Midtown, on the verge of tears, and positive you won't get a decent table, just call them and say you're going to be a little late. The relief you'll feel when they accommodate your situation will wash over you in an awesome wave.

- Unless you're under the gun, never order off the menu.

- Fine dining establishments can make a steak look like art. But it's not art; it's meat. Don't just stare. Eat it.

- Don't shoot yourself in the foot: Not everyone takes credit cards or electronic payments, so it's still important to carry some cash with you. Otherwise, you'll be unable to tip the bouncer to get into a club, pay the bartender in case they don't accept drink tickets, or meet the going rate for nighttime freelance shift workers.

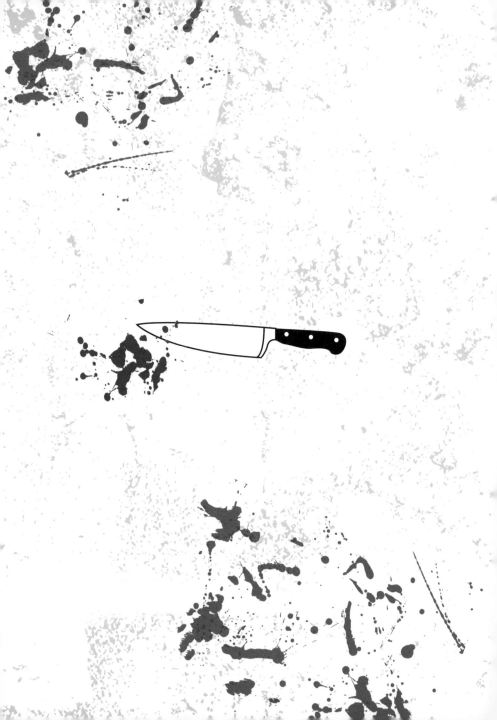

"I know my behavior can be erratic sometimes."

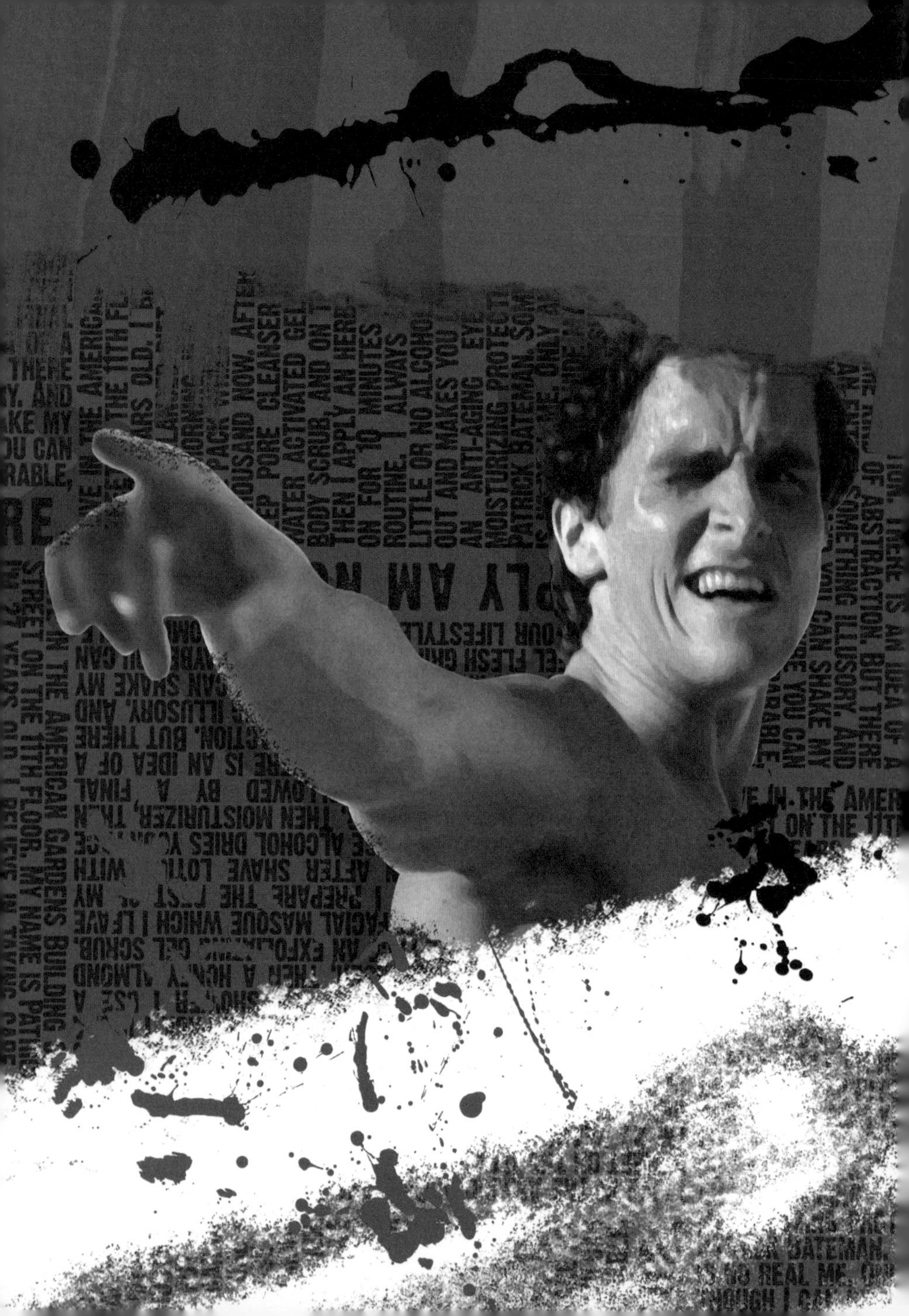

Support women-owned businesses. And reward killer service, especially from those working late shifts, with repeat business.

Nobody goes to a club for conversation. Instead of droning on about how you just want to have a meaningful relationship with someone, slay your companions with your utterly insane sense of style and confidence.

- Remember, nobody will truly ever understand who you are or what you do. And since they won't know the difference between mergers and acquisitions and murders and executions, you might as well slap them in the face with a whole lot of fantastical-sounding truths about yourself.

- Don't be a pushover if the vibe is off and you don't want to do something. Just cancel it.

"There is a moment of sheer panic when I realize that Paul's apartment overlooks the park ... and is obviously more expensive than mine."

HOME:
REST IN PEACE

A VIEW FOR A KILL

Even if you rarely look outside or keep your privacy shades drawn, guests will never fail to be impressed, jealous, or intimidated by a killer view, so insist on large windows. They also offer lots of natural light, which is the most flattering kind.

White vinegar, baking soda, and hydrogen peroxide can help remove stains from fabric. If push comes to shove and none of those work, bring your linens to a dry cleaner you trust, or at least one who won't ask too many questions.

As a leading member of the community and a member of your HOA or condo board, it behooves you to keep abreast of the current real estate scene. Carve out some time to attend open houses to see what's come on the market. Feel free to engage the agent in meaningful conversation regarding the sellers, the building, or the quality of the renovations being done, especially to pre-war apartments. Be sure, however, to not waste their time with inappropriate questions or by arriving uninvited or unannounced if it's a private or managed showing—you might need them when you decide it's time for a new or second home yourself!

● Use the right tool for the right job. Don't use a nail gun when you should be using an ax. Use duct tape for taping something.

"I guess you
could say I just
want to have
a meaningful
relationship
with someone
special."

 Always have a very fine chardonnay on hand for guests to enjoy before you shoot your shot.

When leaving the outgoing message on your voicemail, clearly state your name and the reason you're unable to answer the call. Adding a personal touch, like an aside to your partner, or a punch line like a current pop culture reference, will make you seem more personable and human.

Streaming may be all the rage, but in a world where favorite films or shows can drop off of platforms, or where you may not want the algorithm to know what you're into, it's prudent to invest in physical media. By keeping a well-stocked library of classics on hand, you'll be sure to always have it on hand, even if it's just playing in the background while you're on a work call.

47897 55010

I HAVE

TO RETURN

HORROR

SOME

VIDEOTAPES

● Be kind, rewind, and return your videotapes.

AFTERWORD

So that, reader, is how to be me. But you should know: despite my success, my looks, my life, my pain is constant and sharp and I do not hope for a better world for anyone. Including you. In fact, I want my pain to be inflicted on others. I want no one to escape. But even after admitting this, there is no catharsis. My punishment continues to elude me, and I gain no deeper knowledge of myself; no new knowledge can be extracted from my telling. This confession has meant nothing.

Anyway, thanks for buying this book. Rest assured that the royalties I make will be funneled into fueling my hobbies.

I'll be seeing you. Maybe tomorrow. Maybe at the office, or Harry's Bar. Maybe at Espace, or next to you at a matinee of *Oh Africa, Brave Africa*. Or maybe, maybe, I'm already right behind you.

So, keep your eyes open!

First published in the United States of America in 2025 by
Rizzoli Universe
A Division of Rizzoli International Publications, Inc.
49 West 27th Street
New York, NY 10001
www.rizzoliusa.com

Publisher: Charles Miers
Associate Publisher: Jessica Fuller
Design: Celina Carvalho
Production Manager: Colin Hough-Trapp

ISBN: 978-0-7893-4574-5
Library of Congress Control Number: 2024941643

Printed in China

2025 2026 2027 2028 2029 / 10 9 8 7 6 5 4 3 2 1

Visit us online:
Instagram.com/RizzoliBooks
Facebook.com/RizzoliNewYork
X: @Rizzoli_Books
Youtube.com/user/RizzoliNY

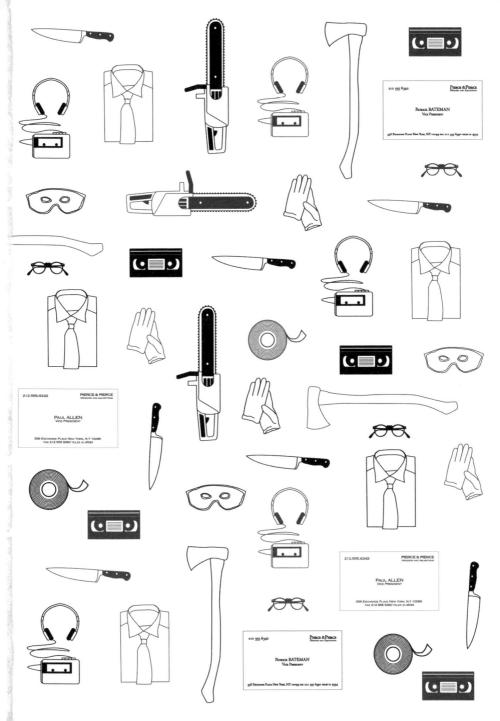

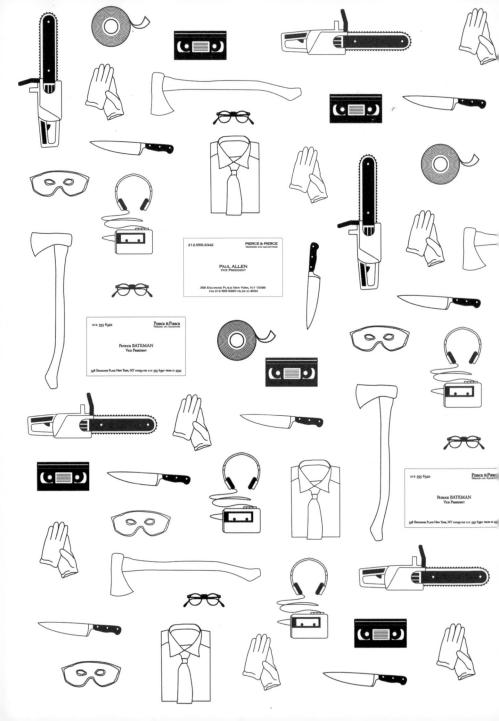